baking

a celebration of the simple joys of baking

This edition published in 2010
LOVE FOOD is an imprint of Parragon Books Ltd

Parragon
Queen Street House
4 Queen Street
Bath BA1 1HE, UK

ISBN: 978-1-4075-4981-1
Printed in China

Photography by Clive Streeter
Food styling by Angela Drake and Teresa Goldfinch
Internal design by Jane Bozzard-Hill
Introduction and additional recipes by Christine France

Notes for the reader
• This book uses both imperial, metric, and U.S. cup measurements. Follow the
same units of measurement throughout; do not mix imperial and metric.
• All spoon measurements are level; teaspoons are assumed to be 5 ml and
tablespoons are assumed to be 15 ml.
• Unless otherwise stated, milk is assumed to be low-fat and eggs are large.
• Some recipes contain nuts. If you are allergic to nuts you should avoid them and
any products containing nuts. Recipes using raw or very lightly cooked eggs should
be avoided by infants, the elderly, pregnant women, convalescents, and anyone
suffering from an illness.

contents

introduction

If you remember as a child coming home to the irresistible smells of baking wafting from the kitchen, then you'll know just how rewarding baking can be. For many of our grandmothers, a baking day was a weekly event, when whole batches of traditional cakes and cookies would be lovingly prepared to stock the pantry to feed hungry families, pack for school lunches, or set out on pretty plates for weekend visitors.

Nowadays, many of us feel that we just don't have the time for home baking and since we can now buy a good variety of packaged cakes and cookies, there's no particular incentive to bake our own. But there's quite simply nothing like freshly home-baked cakes, made with love. You don't even have to spend a whole day baking to get worthwhile results—some cakes take as little as half an hour of your time. However, if you have a freezer, it's often worth making a larger batch of cakes in one session as most cakes freeze successfully (without fillings or frostings) and can be stored for several months.

Even if you've never baked a cake before, you'll be surprised how simple it is. All the instructions you need are given in the recipes, so if you follow the easy steps, you really can't go wrong. Why not revive the baking tradition in your home? Then you'll never be short of a home-baked treat to offer visitors when they drop by.

useful equipment

OVEN

A reliable oven is essential, as temperature is critical for most recipes. You'll need to check regularly that the thermostat is accurate, so consider investing in an oven thermometer. Place it on the middle shelf and preheat the oven for 10–15 minutes before reading.

Ovens do vary, so always check for doneness 5–10 minutes before the end of the cooking time. Similarly, don't worry if your cake takes a little longer to cook than stated in the recipe—just return it to the oven for an additional 5 minutes and check again, repeating if necessary.

MEASURING SPOONS AND CUPS

Unless you're an experienced cook, you should measure all baking ingredients to be sure of success. To measure small amounts, you'll need a set of standard spoon measures—$1/4$, $1/2$, and 1 teaspoon, and 1 tablespoon.

For larger quantities, you'll need a set of standard cup measures—$1/4$, $1/3$, $1/2$, and 1 cup (1 cup = 8 fl oz). Dry ingredients should be smoothed level.

To measure liquids, choose a heatproof glass or plastic measuring cup with clear markings. Place it on a flat surface at eye level to measure accurately.

BAKING PANS

It's worth investing in good-quality bakeware as it will keep its shape, conduct the heat efficiently and evenly to cake mixtures, and last for years. Nonstick pans can make turning out easier, but may not be as durable as uncoated pans. Flexible silicone bakeware is a good alternative to traditional metal pans because it makes the job of removing baked goods from the pan simple and effortless, and is easy to clean.

It important to use the type of pan stated in the recipe. These are the most useful:

- 1–2 cookie sheets
- Deep round and square pans, 7–9 inches/18–23 cm
- 2–3 shallow round layer pans, 7–8 inches/18–20 cm
- Rectangular baking pan
- Springform round pan, for easy removal of delicate cakes and cheesecakes, 8–9 inches/20–23 cm
- Loaf pans, 1 lb/450 g and 2 lb/900 g
- 12-cup muffin pan

MIXING BOWLS

You'll need a selection of different sized mixing bowls for baking, and the easiest to start with is a set of tempered glass mixing bowls, which are tough and easy to clean. If you bake regularly, you may find that you need extra bowls, so you can add the sizes you find most useful. Melamine or plastic bowls often have pouring lips and non-slip bottoms that grip the counter firmly, and are extremely hard-wearing. If your bowl doesn't have a non-slip bottom, place a damp dish towel underneath it to prevent movement.

WHISKS AND MIXERS

A hand-held electric mixer saves a lot of hard work when mixing cake batters, so if you plan to bake regularly, it's another good investment. Most have variable speeds, but can cope with only small quantities of mixture. Make sure you choose a mixer with a powerful motor that will not wear out too quickly.

Stand mixers are good if you plan to mix large amounts as they have more powerful motors and a greater capacity.

A food processor is able to do most creaming and blending jobs and some have an attachment for whipping egg whites.

WIRE COOLING RACK

To cool cakes quickly and evenly, you'll need a simple wire rack to turn them out onto. For a major baking session you can even buy tiered racks, but for most purposes a single rectangular rack is adequate.

WOODEN SPOONS

A choice of different sized wooden spoons is great for any kitchen, and it's a good idea to keep some for specific tasks, as wood can absorb and transfer flavors.

SPATULAS

Flexible plastic or rubber spatulas are useful for scraping cake mixture from mixing bowls. It's good to have a selection of sizes.

A metal spatula makes smoothing and shaping mixtures very easy and can aid the removal of delicate cakes from pans. Choose one with a long, slightly flexible blade and comfortable handle.

SIFTER

A rustproof metal or nylon sifter is used for sifting together flours and dry ingredients, making sure of the even distribution of rising agents and spices in cake mixtures.

ROLLING PIN

Wooden pins are fine for general use, but marble or glass pins are good for rolling out mixtures that need a cool touch.

PASTRY BRUSH

A pastry brush is used for greasing cake pans or brushing glazes onto pastry or cakes. Choose one that can be cleaned easily—some are even dishwasher-proof.

top tips for successful baking

BEFORE YOU START

- Always preheat the oven to the correct temperature so it's ready to use when your cake is mixed. Allow at least 10 minutes for preheating.

- Grease pans lightly with a mild-flavored oil, such as sunflower oil, or melted butter. Use a pastry brush to cover the pan quickly and evenly.

- For creamed mixtures, such as layer cakes, line the bottom of the pan with nonstick parchment paper; for rich mixtures and fruit cakes, line the bottom and sides of the pan. For very rich fruit cakes, wrap a double thickness of brown paper around the outside of the pan for extra protection and tie with string to secure.

- If you don't have the correct-sized pan for the recipe, or prefer to use an unusual shaped pan such as a heart-shaped pan, just match the capacity—e.g. an 8-inch/20-cm round pan holds about the same volume of liquid as a 7-inch/18-cm square pan.

- Assemble all your ingredients and measure everything before you start to mix.

THE PERFECT MIX

- Always sift the flour with rising agents or spices before adding to a mixture so that they are evenly distributed throughout the mix.

- If you run out of self-rising flour, add 2½ teaspoons baking powder to every 2 cups all-purpose flour and sift together thoroughly before use.

- Most cake recipes use either butter or hard (block) margarine, which are interchangeable although butter has a much better flavor. Soft (tub) margarines and oil are good for all-in-one recipes, but less successful for creamed methods. Low-fat spreads have a high water content and give poor results in conventional recipes.

- For most recipes, fats should be used at room temperature for ease of mixing. Hard butter or block margarine can be softened for a few seconds in the microwave to make mixing easier.

- It's best to use eggs at room temperature for baking as they give a better volume and hold more air when whipped. If you usually store your eggs in the refrigerator, remove them about 30 minutes before you start to mix.

- To separate eggs, tap the shell against the side of a mixing bowl to crack, then break open, letting the white run out into the bowl and holding the yolk in one half of the shell. Tip the yolk backward and forward from shell to shell to let all the white run into the bowl.

- When folding in flour, use a metal spoon, cutting through the mixture with a light, quick action to keep as much air in it as possible. Over-mixing can result in a heavy, close-textured cake.

BAKED TO PERFECTION

- Unless otherwise stated, place your cake on the center shelf of the oven to bake. If your oven tends to cook more quickly at the back or sides, carefully turn the cake pan or cookie sheet around toward the end of the cooking time.

- Resist the temptation to open the oven door too often during cooking, and close it gently rather than banging it shut. It's best to try to wait until at least halfway through the cooking time before sneaking a look. A quick peep won't harm the cake, but if you open the door too often, the temperature will drop and this may prevent the cake from rising properly.

- To test light sponge cakes for doneness, press the top lightly with a fingertip—the cake should feel spongy to the touch and spring back when released. To check rich fruit cakes for doneness, listen closely—if the cake is still sizzling inside, it is not yet thoroughly cooked. Most large cakes will shrink slightly from the sides of the pan when they are cooked. As a final test, insert a toothpick or thin knife into the center of the cake, then lift it out. If the cake is cooked, it should come out clean; if it's sticky, the mixture needs more cooking.

- Most cakes should be cooled slightly in the pan before turning out, as they shrink from the sides of the pan and become firmer, so turning out is easier.

- Use a metal cooling rack for cooling cakes to make sure that any excess steam can escape without making the cake soggy. If you don't have a cooling rack, use the rack from a broiler pan or a barbecue rack.

- Always make sure your cake is completely cool before storing, as if any steam remains, it can cause mold. Store cakes for short periods in a ventilated container with a close-fitting lid. Use airtight containers or sealed plastic bags for freezing.

favorite cakes

sponge layer cake

1¼ cups self-rising flour

1 tsp baking powder

¾ cup butter, softened,
    plus extra for greasing

scant 1 cup superfine sugar

3 eggs

FILLING

3 tbsp raspberry jelly

1¼ cups heavy cream, whipped

16 fresh strawberries, halved

confectioners' sugar, for dusting

PREHEAT THE OVEN to 350°F/180°C, then grease and line the bottoms of two 8-inch/20-cm round layer cake pans. Sift the flour and baking powder into a bowl and add the butter, superfine sugar, and eggs. Mix together, then beat well until smooth.

DIVIDE THE MIXTURE evenly between the prepared pans and smooth the surfaces. Bake in the preheated oven for 25–30 minutes, or until well risen and golden brown, and the cakes feel springy when lightly pressed.

LET COOL in the pans for 5 minutes, then turn out and peel off the lining paper. Transfer to wire racks to cool completely. Join the cakes together with the raspberry jelly, whipped heavy cream, and strawberry halves. Dust with confectioners' sugar and serve.

SERVES 8

chocolate fudge cake

³/₄ cup butter, softened, plus extra for
    greasing

heaping 1 cup superfine sugar

3 eggs, beaten

3 tbsp dark corn syrup

3 tbsp ground almonds

heaping 1 cup self-rising flour

pinch of salt

¹/₄ cup unsweetened cocoa

FROSTING

8 oz/225 g semisweet chocolate,
    broken into pieces

¹/₄ cup dark brown sugar

1 cup butter, diced

5 tbsp evaporated milk

¹/₂ tsp vanilla extract

GREASE AND LINE the bottoms of two 8-inch/20-cm round layer cake pans.

TO MAKE THE FROSTING, place the chocolate, brown sugar, butter, evaporated milk, and vanilla extract in a heavy-bottom pan. Heat gently, stirring constantly, until melted. Pour into a bowl and let cool. Cover and let chill in the refrigerator for 1 hour, or until spreadable.

PREHEAT THE OVEN to 350°F/180°C. Place the butter and superfine sugar in a bowl and beat together until light and fluffy. Gradually beat in the eggs. Stir in the corn syrup and ground almonds. Sift the flour, salt, and cocoa into a separate bowl, then fold into the cake batter. Add a little water, if necessary, to make a dropping consistency. Spoon the cake batter into the prepared pans and bake in the oven for 30–35 minutes, or until springy to the touch and the tip of a knife inserted in the center comes out clean.

LET STAND IN THE PANS for 5 minutes, then turn out onto wire racks to cool completely. When the cakes have cooled, sandwich them together with half of the frosting. Spread the remaining frosting over the top and sides of the cake and swirl it with a metal spatula.

SERVES 8

coffee & walnut cake

PREHEAT THE OVEN to 350°F/180°C. Grease and line the bottoms of two 8-inch/20-cm round layer cake pans.

CREAM TOGETHER the butter and brown sugar until pale and fluffy. Gradually add the eggs, beating well after each addition. Beat in the coffee.

SIFT THE FLOUR and baking powder into the mixture, then fold in lightly and evenly with a metal spoon. Fold in the walnut pieces.

DIVIDE THE MIXTURE between the prepared cake pans and smooth level. Bake in the preheated oven for 20–25 minutes, or until golden brown and springy to the touch. Turn out onto a wire rack to cool.

FOR THE FROSTING, beat together the butter, confectioners' sugar, coffee, and vanilla extract, mixing until smooth and creamy.

USE ABOUT HALF of the frosting to sandwich the cakes together, then spread the remaining frosting on top and swirl with a metal spatula. Decorate with walnut halves.

SERVES 8

$^3/_4$ cup butter, plus extra for greasing
$^3/_4$ cup light brown sugar
3 extra large eggs, beaten
3 tbsp strong black coffee
1$^1/_2$ cups self-rising flour
1$^1/_2$ tsp baking powder
1 cup walnut pieces
walnut halves, to decorate

FROSTING
$^1/_2$ cup butter
1$^3/_4$ cups confectioners' sugar
1 tbsp strong black coffee
$^1/_2$ tsp vanilla extract

sticky toffee cake

1 cup chopped, pitted dried dates

$^3/_4$ cup boiling water

$^1/_2$ tsp baking soda

6 tbsp butter, plus extra for greasing

$^3/_4$ cup superfine sugar

1 extra large egg, beaten

$^1/_2$ tsp vanilla extract

$1^1/_2$ cups self-rising flour

TOFFEE SAUCE

$^1/_3$ cup light brown sugar

3 tbsp butter

2 tbsp light cream or milk

PREHEAT THE OVEN to 350°F/180°C. Grease and line an 8-inch/20-cm square cake pan.

PUT THE CHOPPED DATES into a small pan with the boiling water and baking soda. Heat gently for about 5 minutes, without boiling, until the dates are soft.

CREAM TOGETHER the butter and superfine sugar in a bowl until light and fluffy. Beat in the egg, vanilla extract, and date mixture.

FOLD IN THE FLOUR using a metal spoon, mixing evenly. Pour the mixture into the prepared cake pan. Bake in the preheated oven for 40–45 minutes, or until firm to the touch and just starting to shrink away from sides of pan.

FOR THE TOFFEE SAUCE, combine the brown sugar, butter, and cream in a pan and heat gently until melted. Simmer gently, stirring, for about 2 minutes.

REMOVE THE CAKE from the oven and prick all over the surface with a skewer or fork. Pour the hot toffee sauce evenly over the surface. Let cool in the pan, then cut into squares.

SERVES 9

carrot cake with cream cheese frosting

¾ cup sunflower oil, plus extra
    for greasing
¾ cup light brown sugar
3 eggs, beaten
1¼ cups grated carrots
⅔ cup golden raisins
½ cup walnut pieces
grated rind of 1 orange
1½ cups self-rising flour
1 tsp baking soda
1 tsp ground cinnamon
½ tsp grated nutmeg
strips of orange zest, to decorate

FROSTING
scant 1 cup cream cheese
scant 1 cup confectioner's sugar
2 tsp orange juice

PREHEAT THE OVEN to 350°F/180°C. Grease and line the bottom of a 9-inch/23-cm square cake pan.

IN A LARGE BOWL beat together the oil, brown sugar, and eggs. Stir in the grated carrots, golden raisins, walnuts, and orange rind.

SIFT TOGETHER the flour, baking soda, cinnamon, and nutmeg, then stir evenly into the carrot mixture.

SPOON THE MIXTURE into the prepared cake pan and bake in the preheated oven for 40–45 minutes, until well risen and firm to the touch.

REMOVE THE CAKE from the oven and set on a wire rack for 5 minutes. Turn the cake out to cool completely.

FOR THE FROSTING, combine the cream cheese, confectioner's sugar, and orange juice in a bowl and beat until smooth. Spread over the cake and swirl with a metal spatula. Decorate with strips of orange zest and serve cut into squares.

SERVES 16

caribbean coconut cake

PREHEAT THE OVEN to 350°F/180°C. Grease and line the bottoms of two 8-inch/20-cm round layer cake pans. Place ¾ cup of the butter in a bowl with the superfine sugar and eggs, and sift in the flour, baking powder, and nutmeg. Beat together until smooth, then stir in the coconut and 2 tablespoons of the coconut cream.

DIVIDE THE MIXTURE between the prepared pans and smooth the tops. Bake in the preheated oven for 25 minutes, or until golden and firm to the touch. Let cool in the pans for 5 minutes, then turn out onto a wire rack, peel off the lining paper, and let cool completely.

SIFT THE CONFECTIONERS' SUGAR into a bowl and add the remaining butter and coconut cream. Beat together until smooth. Spread the pineapple jelly on one of the cakes and top with just under half of the buttercream. Place the other cake on top. Spread the remaining buttercream on top of the cake and scatter with the toasted coconut.

SERVES 10

1¼ cups butter, softened, plus extra
   for greasing
scant 1 cup superfine sugar
3 eggs
1¼ cups self-rising flour
1½ tsp baking powder
½ tsp freshly grated nutmeg
⅔ cup dry unsweetened coconut
5 tbsp coconut cream
2¾ cups confectioners' sugar
5 tbsp pineapple jelly
dry unsweetened coconut, toasted,
   to decorate

strawberry roulade

3 eggs

²/₃ cup superfine sugar

scant 1 cup all-purpose flour

1 tbsp hot water

1 tbsp toasted slivered almonds,
   to decorate

FILLING

³/₄ cup low-fat mascarpone cheese

1 tsp almond extract

1¹/₂ cups small strawberries

PREHEAT THE OVEN to 425°F/220°C. Line a 14 × 10-inch/35 × 25-cm jelly roll pan with parchment paper.

PLACE THE EGGS in a heatproof bowl with the superfine sugar. Place the bowl over a pan of hot water and whisk until pale and thick.

REMOVE THE BOWL from the pan. Sift in the flour and fold into the egg mixture along with the hot water. Pour the mixture into the prepared pan and bake in the preheated oven for 8–10 minutes, until golden and springy to the touch.

TURN OUT THE CAKE onto a sheet of parchment paper. Peel off the lining paper and roll up the sponge cake tightly along with the parchment paper. Wrap in a clean dish cloth and let cool.

FOR THE FILLING, mix together the mascarpone cheese and the almond extract. Wash, hull, and slice the strawberries. Chill the mascarpone mixture and the strawberries in the refrigerator until ready to use.

UNROLL THE CAKE, spread the mascarpone mixture over the surface, and sprinkle with sliced strawberries. Roll the cake up again (without the parchment paper this time) and transfer to a serving plate. Sprinkle with slivered almonds and serve.

SERVES 8

baked lemon cheesecake

¹/₄ cup butter, plus extra for greasing

3 cups crushed gingersnaps

3 lemons

1¹/₃ cups ricotta cheese

scant 1 cup strained plain yogurt

4 eggs

1 tbsp cornstarch

¹/₂ cup superfine sugar

strips of lemon zest, to decorate

confectioners' sugar, for dusting

PREHEAT THE OVEN to 350°F/180°C. Lightly grease an 8-inch/20-cm round springform pan and line the bottom with nonstick parchment paper.

MELT THE BUTTER and stir in the cookie crumbs. Press into the base of the prepared cake pan. Chill until firm.

MEANWHILE, finely grate the rind and squeeze the juice from the lemons. Add the ricotta, yogurt, eggs, cornstarch, and superfine sugar and whip until a smooth batter is formed.

CAREFULLY POUR the mixture into the pan. Bake in the preheated oven for 40–45 minutes, or until just firm and golden brown.

COOL THE CHEESECAKE completely in the pan, then run a knife around the edge to loosen, and turn out onto a serving plate. Decorate with lemon zest and dust with confectioners' sugar.

SERVES 6-8

plum crumble tart

PREHEAT THE OVEN to 350°F/180°C and preheat a cookie sheet.

SIFT THE FLOUR, cornstarch, and baking powder into a large bowl and rub in the butter using your fingertips until it resembles fine breadcrumbs. Stir in the hazelnuts and sugar, with just enough milk to bind together.

REMOVE about a quarter of the mixture, cover, and place in the refrigerator. Gently knead together the remainder and press into the base and sides of an 8-inch/20-cm round tart pan with a loose base.

FOR THE FILLING, halve and pit the plums, cut into quarters, and toss with the cornstarch, sugar, and orange rind. Arrange the plums over the dough.

REMOVE THE RESERVED DOUGH from the refrigerator and, using your fingertips, crumble over the plums.

PLACE THE TART on the cookie sheet and bake in the preheated oven for 40–45 minutes, until lightly browned and bubbling. Serve warm or cold.

SERVES 8–10

DOUGH

1 1/2 cups all-purpose flour

1 tbsp cornstarch

1/2 tsp baking powder

7 tbsp butter

1/3 cup finely chopped hazelnuts

scant 1/4 cup superfine sugar

2–3 tbsp milk

FILLING

400 g/14 oz ripe red plums

1 tbsp cornstarch

3 tbsp superfine sugar

finely grated rind of 1 small orange

pecan pie

PIE DOUGH

1³/₄ cups all-purpose flour, plus extra
    for dusting
¹/₂ cup butter
2 tbsp superfine sugar
a little cold water

FILLING

5 tbsp butter
scant ¹/₂ cup light brown sugar
²/₃ cup dark corn syrup
2 extra large eggs, beaten
1 tsp vanilla extract
1 cup pecan nuts

FOR THE PIE DOUGH, place the flour in a bowl and rub in the butter using your fingertips until it resembles fine breadcrumbs. Stir in the superfine sugar and add enough cold water to mix to a firm dough. Wrap in plastic wrap and chill for 15 minutes, until firm enough to roll out.

PREHEAT THE OVEN to 400°F/200°C. Roll out the dough on a lightly floured counter and use to line a 9-inch/23-cm round tart pan with a loose bottom. Prick the base with a fork. Chill for 15 minutes.

PLACE THE TART PAN on a cookie sheet and line with a sheet of parchment paper and pie weights. Bake blind in the preheated oven for 10 minutes. Remove the pie weights and parchment paper and bake for an additional 5 minutes. Reduce the oven temperature to 350°F/180°C.

FOR THE FILLING, place the butter, brown sugar, and corn syrup in a pan and heat gently until melted. Remove from the heat and quickly beat in the eggs and vanilla extract.

COARSELY CHOP the pecan nuts and stir into the mixture. Pour into the tart shell and bake for 35–40 minutes, until the filling is just set. Serve warm or cold.

SERVES 8

everyday cakes & bakes

apple pie

PIE DOUGH

2½ cups all-purpose flour

pinch of salt

6 tbsp butter or margarine,
   cut into small pieces

6 tbsp lard or vegetable shortening,
   cut into small pieces

about 6 tbsp cold water

beaten egg or milk, for glazing

FILLING

1 lb 10 oz–2 lb 4 oz/750 g–1 kg
   baking apples, peeled, cored, and
   sliced

scant ²/₃ cup light brown sugar or
   superfine sugar, plus extra for
   sprinkling

½–1 tsp ground cinnamon, allspice,
   or ground ginger

1–2 tbsp water (optional)

TO MAKE THE PIE DOUGH, sift the flour and salt into a large bowl. Add the butter and lard and rub in using your fingertips until the mixture resembles fine breadcrumbs. Add the water and gather the mixture together into a dough. Wrap the dough and let chill in the refrigerator for 30 minutes.

PREHEAT THE OVEN to 425°F/220°C. Roll out almost two thirds of the pie dough thinly and use to line a deep 9-inch/23-cm pie plate or pie pan.

MIX THE APPLES with the sugar and spice and pack into the pastry shell; the filling can come up above the rim. Add the water if needed, particularly if the apples are a dry variety.

ROLL OUT the remaining pie dough to form a lid. Dampen the edges of the pie rim with water and position the lid, pressing the edges firmly together. Trim and crimp the edges.

USE THE TRIMMINGS to cut out leaves or other shapes to decorate the top of the pie. Dampen and attach. Glaze the top of the pie with beaten egg or milk, make 1 or 2 slits in the top, and place the pie on a baking sheet.

BAKE IN THE PREHEATED OVEN for 20 minutes, then reduce the temperature to 350°F/180°C and bake for an additional 30 minutes, or until the pastry is a light golden brown. Serve hot or cold, sprinkled with sugar.

SERVES 6-8

lemon meringue pie

PIE DOUGH

heaping 1 cup all-purpose flour,
    plus extra for dusting

6 tbsp butter, cut into small pieces,
    plus extra for greasing

$1/4$ cup confectioners' sugar, sifted

finely grated rind of $1/2$ lemon

$1/2$ egg yolk, beaten

$1 1/2$ tbsp milk

FILLING

3 tbsp cornstarch

$1 1/4$ cups water

juice and grated rind of 2 lemons

heaping $3/4$ cup superfine sugar

2 eggs, separated

TO MAKE THE PIE DOUGH, sift the flour into a bowl. Rub in the butter using your fingertips until the mixture resembles fine breadcrumbs. Mix in the remaining ingredients. Knead briefly on a lightly floured counter. Let rest for 30 minutes.

PREHEAT THE OVEN to 350°F/180°C. Grease an 8-inch/20-cm round tart pan with butter. Roll out the pie dough to a thickness of $1/4$ inch/5 mm and use it to line the bottom and sides of the pan. Prick all over with a fork, line with parchment paper, and fill with pie weights. Bake in the preheated oven for 15 minutes. Remove from the oven and take out the parchment paper and pie weights. Reduce the temperature to 300°F/150°C.

TO MAKE THE FILLING, mix the cornstarch with a little of the water. Place the remaining water in a pan. Stir in the lemon juice and rind and cornstarch paste. Bring to a boil, stirring. Cook for 2 minutes. Let cool a little. Stir in 5 tablespoons of the superfine sugar and the egg yolks, then pour into the pastry shell.

WHIP THE EGG WHITES in a clean, greasefree bowl until stiff. Whip in the remaining superfine sugar and spread over the pie. Bake for another 40 minutes. Remove from the oven, cool, and serve.

SERVES 6-8

double chocolate brownies

PREHEAT THE OVEN to 350°F/180°C. Grease and line the bottom of a 7-inch/18-cm square cake pan. Place the butter and chocolate in a small heatproof bowl set over a saucepan of gently simmering water until melted. Stir until smooth. Let cool slightly. Stir in the sugar, salt, and vanilla extract. Add the eggs, one at a time, stirring well, until blended.

SIFT THE FLOUR and cocoa into the cake batter and beat until smooth. Stir in the chocolate chips, then pour the batter into the prepared pan. Bake in the preheated oven for 35–40 minutes, or until the top is evenly colored and a toothpick inserted into the center comes out almost clean. Let cool slightly while preparing the sauce.

TO MAKE THE SAUCE, place the butter, sugar, milk, cream, and corn syrup in a small saucepan and heat gently until the sugar has dissolved. Bring to a boil and stir for 10 minutes, or until the mixture is caramel-colored. Remove from the heat and add the chocolate. Stir until smooth. Cut the brownies into squares and serve immediately with the sauce.

makes 9

1/2 cup butter, plus extra
    for greasing
4 oz/115 g semisweet chocolate,
    broken into pieces
1 1/3 cups superfine sugar
pinch of salt
1 tsp vanilla extract
2 eggs
1 cup all-purpose flour
2 tbsp unsweetened cocoa
1/2 cup white chocolate chips

FUDGE SAUCE
4 tbsp butter
heaping 1 cup superfine sugar
2/3 cup milk
heaping 1 cup heavy cream
2/3 cup dark corn syrup
7 oz/200 g semisweet chocolate,
    broken into pieces

classic cherry cake

heaping 1 cup candied cherries,
    quartered
³/₄ cup ground almonds
1³/₄ cups all-purpose flour
1 tsp baking powder
scant 1 cup butter, plus extra for
    greasing
1 cup superfine sugar
3 extra large eggs
finely grated rind and juice of
    1 lemon
6 sugar cubes, crushed

PREHEAT THE OVEN to 350°F/180°C. Grease an 8-inch/20-cm round cake pan and line the bottom and sides with nonstick parchment paper.

STIR TOGETHER the candied cherries, ground almonds, and 1 tablespoon of the flour. Sift the remaining flour into a separate bowl with the baking powder.

CREAM TOGETHER the butter and sugar until light in color and fluffy in texture. Gradually add the eggs, beating hard with each addition, until evenly mixed.

ADD THE FLOUR MIXTURE and fold lightly and evenly into the creamed mixture with a metal spoon. Add the cherry mixture and fold in evenly. Finally, fold in the lemon rind and juice.

SPOON THE MIXTURE into the prepared cake pan and sprinkle with the crushed sugar cubes. Bake in the preheated oven for 1–1¼ hours, or until risen, golden brown, and the cake is just beginning to shrink away from the sides of the pan.

COOL IN THE PAN for about 15 minutes, then turn out to finish cooling on a wire rack.

SERVES 8

gingerbread

³/₄ cup butter, plus extra
  for greasing
heaping ²/₃ cup dark brown sugar
³/₄ cup light corn syrup
finely grated rind and juice of
  1 small orange
2 extra large eggs, beaten
2 cups self-rising flour
scant ¹/₂ cup whole wheat flour
2 tsp ground ginger
3 tbsp chopped candied ginger or
  preserved ginger
pieces of candied ginger or
  preserved ginger, to decorate

PREHEAT THE OVEN to 350°F/180°C. Grease a 9-inch/23-cm square deep cake pan and line the bottom with nonstick parchment paper.

PLACE THE BUTTER, sugar, and corn syrup in a pan and heat gently, stirring until melted. Remove from the heat.

BEAT IN the orange rind and juice, eggs, flours, and ground ginger, then beat thoroughly to mix evenly. Stir in the chopped candied ginger.

SPOON THE BATTER into the prepared pan and bake in the preheated oven for 40–45 minutes, or until risen and firm to the touch.

COOL IN THE PAN for about 10 minutes, then turn out and finish cooling on a wire rack. Cut into squares and decorate with pieces of candied ginger.

SERVES 9

devil's food cake

PREHEAT THE OVEN to 325°F/170°C. Grease two 8-inch/20-cm round layer cake pans and line the bottoms with nonstick parchment paper.

BREAK UP THE CHOCOLATE and place with the milk and cocoa in a heatproof bowl set over over a pan of gently simmering water, stirring until melted and smooth. Remove from the heat.

IN A LARGE BOWL, beat together the butter and brown sugar until pale and fluffy. Beat in the egg yolks, then the sour cream and melted chocolate mixture. Sift in the flour and baking soda, then fold in evenly. In a separate bowl, whip the egg whites until stiff enough to hold firm peaks. Fold into the mixture lightly and evenly.

DIVIDE THE MIXTURE between the prepared cake pans, smooth the surface, and bake in the preheated oven for 35–40 minutes, or until risen and firm to the touch. Cool in the pans for 10 minutes, then turn out onto a wire rack.

FOR THE FROSTING, place the chocolate, cocoa, sour cream, corn syrup, butter, and water in a pan and heat gently without boiling, until melted. Remove from the heat and add the confectioners' sugar, stirring until smooth. Cool, stirring occasionally, until the mixture begins to thicken and hold its shape. Split the cakes in half horizontally with a sharp knife to make four layers. Sandwich the cakes together with about a third of the frosting. Spread the remainder over the top and sides of the cakes, swirling with a metal spatula.

5 oz/140 g semisweet chocolate

scant $^1/_2$ cup milk

2 tbsp unsweetened cocoa

$^2/_3$ cup butter, plus extra for greasing

$^2/_3$ cup light brown sugar

3 eggs, separated

4 tbsp sour cream

1$^3/_4$ cups all-purpose flour

1 tsp baking soda

FROSTING

5 oz/140 g semisweet chocolate

$^1/_3$ cup unsweetened cocoa

4 tbsp sour cream

1 tbsp dark corn syrup

3 tbsp butter

4 tbsp water

1$^3/_4$ cups confectioners' sugar

SERVES 8-10

rich fruit cake

scant 2¹/₂ cups golden raisins

1²/₃ cups raisins

¹/₂ cup chopped plumped dried
 apricots

¹/₂ cup chopped pitted dates

4 tbsp dark rum or brandy, plus
 extra for flavoring (optional)

finely grated rind and juice of
 1 orange

1 cup butter, plus extra for greasing

1 cup light brown sugar

4 eggs

generous ¹/₃ chopped candied peel

¹/₃ cup candied cherries, quartered

2 tbsp chopped candied ginger
 or preserved ginger

¹/₃ cup chopped blanched almonds

1³/₄ cups all-purpose flour

1 tsp apple pie spice

PLACE THE GOLDEN RAISINS, raisins, apricots, and dates in a large bowl and stir in the rum, orange rind, and orange juice. Cover and let soak for several hours or overnight.

PREHEAT THE OVEN to 300°F/150°C. Grease and line an 8-inch/20-cm round deep cake pan.

CREAM TOGETHER the butter and sugar until light and fluffy. Gradually beat in the eggs, beating hard after each addition. Stir in the soaked fruits, candied peel, candied cherries, candied ginger, and blanched almonds.

SIFT THE FLOUR AND APPLE PIE SPICE, then fold lightly and evenly into the mixture. Spoon the mixture into the prepared cake pan and level the surface, making a slight depression in the center with the back of the spoon.

BAKE IN THE PREHEATED OVEN for 2¹/₄–2³/₄ hours, or until the cake is beginning to shrink away from the sides of the pan and a toothpick inserted into the center comes out clean. Cool completely in the pan.

TURN OUT THE CAKE and remove the lining paper. Wrap with waxed paper and foil and store for at least 2 months before use. To add a richer flavor, prick the cake with a toothpick and spoon over a couple of tablespoons of extra rum or brandy, if using, before storing.

SERVES 16

chocolate & vanilla marbled loaf

2 oz/55 g semisweet chocolate

3 tbsp milk

5 tbsp butter, plus extra for greasing

scant 1/2 cup superfine sugar

1 egg, beaten

3 tbsp sour cream

1 cup self-rising flour, plus extra
    for dusting

1/2 tsp baking powder

1/2 tsp vanilla extract

PREHEAT THE OVEN to 325°F/170°C. Grease a 1-lb/450-g loaf pan and line the botom with nonstick parchment paper. Dust a little flour around the inside of the pan, shaking out the excess.

BREAK UP THE CHOCOLATE, place it in a small heatproof bowl with the milk, and set the bowl over a pan of simmering water. Heat gently until just melted. Remove from the heat.

CREAM TOGETHER the butter and sugar until light and fluffy. Beat in the egg and sour cream. Sift the flour and baking powder over the mixture, then fold in lightly and evenly using a metal spoon.

SPOON HALF THE MIXTURE into a separate bowl and stir in the chocolate mixture. Add the vanilla extract to the plain mix.

SPOON THE CHOCOLATE and vanilla mixtures alternately into the prepared loaf pan, swirling lightly with a knife or skewer for a marbled effect. Bake in the preheated oven for 40–45 minutes, or until well risen and firm to the touch.

COOL IN THE PAN for 10 minutes, then turn out, and finish cooling on a wire rack.

SERVES 8

banana loaf

PREHEAT THE OVEN Preheat the oven to 350°F/180°C. Lightly grease and line a 2-lb/900-g loaf pan.

SIFT THE FLOURS, sugar, salt, and the spices into a large bowl.

IN A SEPARATE BOWL, mash the bananas with the orange juice, then stir in the eggs and oil. Pour into the dry ingredients and mix well.

SPOON INTO THE PREPARED LOAF PAN and bake in the preheated oven for 1 hour, then test to see if the loaf is cooked by inserting a skewer into the center. If it comes out clean, the loaf is done. If not, bake for an additional 10 minutes and test again.

REMOVE FROM THE OVEN and let cool in the pan. Turn the loaf out, slice, and serve.

SERVES 8

butter, for greasing

scant 1 cup white self-rising flour

scant $^3/_4$ cup light brown
self-rising flour

heaping $^3/_4$ cup raw brown sugar

pinch of salt

$^1/_2$ tsp ground cinnamon

$^1/_2$ tsp ground nutmeg

2 large ripe bananas, peeled

$^3/_4$ cup orange juice

2 eggs, beaten

4 tbsp canola oil

date & walnut loaf

heaping $^1/_2$ cup chopped pitted dates

$^1/_2$ tsp baking soda

finely grated rind of $^1/_2$ lemon

scant $^1/_2$ cup hot tea

3 tbsp butter, plus extra
for greasing

$^1/_3$ cup light brown sugar

1 medium egg

heaping 1 cup self-rising flour

$^1/_4$ cup chopped walnuts

walnut halves, to decorate

PREHEAT THE OVEN to 350°F/180°C. Grease a 1-lb/450-g loaf pan and line the bottom with nonstick parchment paper.

PLACE THE DATES, baking soda, and lemon rind in a bowl and add the hot tea. Let soak for 10 minutes, until softened.

CREAM TOGETHER the butter and sugar until light and fluffy, then beat in the egg. Stir in the date mixture.

FOLD IN THE FLOUR using a large metal spoon, then fold in the chopped walnuts. Spoon the mixture into the prepared cake pan and spread evenly. Top with walnut halves.

BAKE IN THE PREHEATED OVEN for 35–40 minutes, or until risen, firm, and golden brown. Cool for 10 minutes in the pan, then turn out the loaf, and finish cooling on a wire rack.

SERVES 8

cookies & bars

chocolate chip cookies

1½ cups all-purpose flour

1 tsp baking powder

½ cup soft margarine, plus extra for greasing

½ cup light brown sugar

¼ cup superfine sugar

½ tsp vanilla extract

1 egg

⅔ cup semisweet chocolate chips

PREHEAT THE OVEN to 375°F/190°C. Lightly grease 2 cookie sheets.

PLACE ALL OF THE INGREDIENTS in a large mixing bowl and beat until thoroughly combined.

PLACE TABLESPOONFULS of the mixture on to the cookie sheets, spacing them well apart to allow for spreading during cooking.

BAKE IN THE PREHEATED OVEN for 10–12 minutes, or until the cookies are golden brown.

USING A SPATULA, transfer the cookies to a wire rack to cool completely.

makes 30

classic oatmeal cookies

3/4 cup butter or margarine, plus
    extra for greasing
scant 1 1/3 cups raw brown sugar
1 egg
4 tbsp water
1 tsp vanilla extract
4 1/3 cups rolled oats
1 cup all-purpose flour
1 tsp salt
1/2 tsp baking soda

PREHEAT THE OVEN to 350°F/180°C and grease a large cookie sheet.

CREAM THE BUTTER and sugar together in a large mixing bowl. Beat in the egg, water, and vanilla extract until the mixture is smooth.

IN A SEPARATE BOWL, mix the oats, flour, salt, and baking soda. Gradually stir the oat mixture into the butter mixture until thoroughly combined.

PUT TABLESPOONFULS of the mixture onto the greased cookie sheet, making sure they are well spaced. Transfer to the preheated oven and bake for 15 minutes, or until the cookies are golden brown.

REMOVE THE COOKIES from the oven and place on a wire rack to cool before serving.

MAKES 30

peanut butter cookies

PREHEAT THE OVEN to 350°F/180°C, then grease 3 cookie sheets.

PLACE THE BUTTER and peanut butter in a bowl and beat together. Beat in the superfine sugar and brown sugar, then gradually beat in the egg and vanilla extract.

SIFT THE FLOUR, baking soda, baking powder, and salt into the bowl and stir in the oats.

PLACE SPOONFULS of the cookie dough onto the cookie sheets, spaced well apart to allow for spreading. Flatten slightly with a fork.

BAKE IN THE PREHEATED OVEN for 12 minutes, or until lightly browned. Let cool on the cookie sheets for 2 minutes, then transfer to wire racks to cool completely.

makes 26

$^1/_2$ cup butter, softened,
    plus extra for greasing
scant $^1/_2$ cup crunchy peanut butter
heaping $^1/_2$ cup superfine sugar
heaping $^1/_2$ cup light brown sugar
1 egg, beaten
$^1/_2$ tsp vanilla extract
$^2/_3$ cup all-purpose flour
$^1/_2$ tsp baking soda
$^1/_2$ tsp baking powder
pinch of salt
$1^1/_2$ cups rolled oats

gingersnaps

2¹/₂ cups self-rising flour

pinch of salt

1 cup superfine sugar

1 tbsp ground ginger

1 tsp baking soda

¹/₂ cup butter, plus extra for greasing

¹/₄ cup dark corn syrup

1 egg, lightly beaten

1 tsp grated orange rind

PREHEAT THE OVEN to 325°F/160°C. Lightly grease several cookie sheets.

SIFT TOGETHER THE FLOUR, salt, sugar, ground ginger, and baking soda into a large mixing bowl.

HEAT THE BUTTER AND CORN SYRUP together in a pan over very low heat until the butter has melted.

LET THE BUTTER MIXTURE cool slightly, then pour it onto the dry ingredients. Add the egg and orange rind and mix together thoroughly.

USING YOUR HANDS, carefully shape the dough into 30 even-size balls. Place the balls well apart on the prepared cookie sheets, then flatten them slightly with your fingers.

BAKE IN THE PREHEATED OVEN for 15–20 minutes. Carefully transfer the cookies to a wire rack to cool and crisp.

MAKES 30

shortbread

scant 1½ cups all-purpose flour, plus
    extra for dusting
pinch of salt
¼ cup superfine sugar, plus extra for
    sprinkling
¾ cup butter, cut into small pieces,
    plus extra for greasing

PREHEAT THE OVEN to 300°F/150°C. Grease an 8-inch/20-cm fluted round tart pan.

MIX TOGETHER THE FLOUR, salt, and sugar. Rub the butter into the dry ingredients. Continue to work the mixture until it forms a soft dough. Make sure you do not overwork the shortbread or it will be tough, not crumbly as it should be.

LIGHTLY PRESS THE DOUGH into the tart pan. If you don't have a fluted pan, roll out the dough on a lightly floured board, place on a cookie sheet, and pinch the edges to form a scalloped pattern.

MARK INTO 8 PIECES with a knife. Prick all over with a fork and bake in the center of the oven for 45–50 minutes until the shortbread is firm and just colored.

LET COOL in the pan and sprinkle with the sugar. Cut into portions and remove to a wire rack.

makes 8

coconut bars

PREHEAT THE OVEN to 350°F/180°C. Grease a 9-inch/23-cm square cake pan and line the bottom with nonstick parchment paper.

CREAM TOGETHER the butter and superfine sugar until pale and fluffy, then gradually beat in the eggs. Stir in the orange rind, orange juice, and sour cream. Fold in the flour and dry unsweetened coconut evenly using a metal spoon.

SPOON THE MIXTURE into the prepared cake pan and level the surface. Bake in the preheated oven for 35–40 minutes, or until risen and firm to the touch.

LET COOL for 10 minutes in the pan, then turn out, and finish cooling on a wire rack.

FOR THE FROSTING, lightly beat the egg white, just enough to break it up, and stir in the confectioners' sugar and dry unsweetened coconut, adding enough orange juice to mix to a thick paste. Spread over the top of the cake, sprinkle with long shred coconut, then let set before slicing into bars.

makes 10

heaping $\frac{1}{2}$ cup butter, plus extra for
    greasing
heaping 1 cup superfine sugar
2 eggs, beaten
finely grated rind of 1 orange
3 tbsp orange juice
$\frac{2}{3}$ cup sour cream
$1\frac{1}{4}$ cups self-rising flour
1 cup dry unsweetened coconut
toasted long shred coconut,
    to decorate

FROSTING

1 egg white
$1\frac{3}{4}$ cups confectioners' sugar
1 cup dry unsweetened coconut
about 1 tbsp orange juice

almond & raspberry bars

DOUGH

1½ cups all-purpose flour

heaping ½ cup butter

2 tbsp superfine sugar

1 egg yolk

about 1 tbsp cold water

FILLING

½ cup butter

heaping ½ cup superfine sugar

1 cup ground almonds

3 eggs, beaten

½ tsp almond extract

4 tbsp raspberry jelly

2 tbsp slivered almonds

FOR THE DOUGH, sift the flour into a bowl and rub in the butter with your fingertips until the mixture resembles fine breadcrumbs. Stir in the sugar, then combine the egg yolk and water, and stir in to make a firm dough, adding a little more water if necessary. Wrap in plastic wrap and chill in the refrigerator for about 15 minutes, until firm enough to roll out.

PREHEAT THE OVEN to 400°F/200°C. Roll out the dough and use to line a 9-inch/23-cm square tart pan or shallow cake pan. Prick the bottom and chill for 15 minutes.

FOR THE FILLING, cream together the butter and sugar until pale and fluffy, then beat in the ground almonds, eggs, and almond extract.

SPREAD THE JELLY over the bottom of the pastry shell, then top with the almond filling, spreading it evenly. Sprinkle with the slivered almonds.

BAKE IN THE PREHEATED OVEN for 10 minutes, then reduce the temperature to 350°F/180°C, and bake for an additional 25–30 minutes, or until the filling is golden brown and firm to the touch.

COOL IN THE PAN, then cut into bars.

makes 12

lemon drizzle bars

2 eggs

heaping ¾ cup superfine sugar

⅔ cup soft margarine, plus extra for
   greasing

finely grated rind of 1 lemon

1½ cup self-rising flour

½ cup milk

confectioners' sugar, for dusting

SYRUP

1¼ cups confectioners' sugar

¼ cup fresh lemon juice

PREHEAT THE OVEN to 350°F/180°C. Grease a 7-inch/18-cm square cake pan and line with nonstick parchment paper.

PLACE THE EGGS, superfine sugar, and margarine in a bowl and beat hard until smooth and fluffy. Stir in the lemon rind, then fold in the flour lightly and evenly. Stir in the milk, mixing evenly, then spoon into the prepared cake pan, smoothing level.

BAKE IN THE PREHEATED OVEN for 45–50 minutes, or until golden brown and firm to the touch. Remove from the oven and stand the pan on a cooling rack.

TO MAKE THE SYRUP, place the confectioners' sugar and lemon juice in a small pan and heat gently, stirring until the sugar dissolves. Do not boil.

PRICK THE WARM CAKE all over with a fork and spoon the hot syrup evenly over the top, letting it be absorbed.

LET COOL COMPLETELY in the pan, then turn out the cake, cut into 12 pieces, and dust with a little confectioners' sugar before serving.

makes 12

chocolate caramel shortbread

PREHEAT THE OVEN to 350°F/180°C. Grease and line the bottom of a 9-inch/23-cm shallow square cake pan. Place the butter, flour, and sugar in a food processor and process until the mixture starts to bind together. Press into the pan and level the top. Bake in the preheated oven for 20–25 minutes, or until golden.

TO MAKE THE CARAMEL, place the butter, sugar, corn syrup, and condensed milk in a heavy-bottom pan. Heat gently until the sugar has melted. Bring to a boil, then reduce the heat and let simmer for 6–8 minutes, stirring, until very thick. Pour over the shortbread and let chill in the refrigerator for 2 hours, or until firm.

MELT THE CHOCOLATE AND LET COOL, then spread over the caramel. Let chill in the refrigerator for 2 hours, or until set. Cut the shortbread into 12 pieces using a sharp knife and serve.

makes 12

$^1/_2$ cup butter, plus extra
    for greasing
heaping 1 cup all-purpose flour
heaping $^1/_4$ cup superfine sugar
7 oz/200 g semisweet chocolate,
    broken into pieces

CARAMEL
$^3/_4$ cup butter
heaping $^1/_2$ cup superfine sugar
3 tbsp dark corn syrup
14 oz/400 g canned condensed milk

nutty oat bars

scant 2¾ cups rolled oats

¾ cup chopped hazelnuts

6 tbsp all-purpose flour

½ cup butter, plus extra for greasing

2 tbsp dark corn syrup

scant ½ cup light brown sugar

PREHEAT THE OVEN to 350°F/180°C. Grease a 9-inch/23-cm square cake pan. Place the rolled oats, chopped hazelnuts, and flour in a large mixing bowl and stir together.

PLACE THE BUTTER, corn syrup, and sugar in a pan over low heat and stir until melted. Pour onto the dry ingredients and mix well. Turn into the prepared cake pan and smooth the surface with the back of a spoon.

BAKE IN THE PREHEATED OVEN for 20–25 minutes, or until golden and firm to the touch. Mark into 16 pieces and let cool in the pan. When completely cooled, cut through with a sharp knife and remove from the pan.

MAKES 16

small cakes

low-fat blueberry muffins

heaping 1½ cups all-purpose flour

1 tsp baking soda

¼ tsp salt

1 tsp allspice

heaping ½ cup superfine sugar

3 egg whites

3 tbsp low-fat margarine

⅔ cup thick low-fat plain yogurt or
blueberry-flavored yogurt

1 tsp vanilla extract

¾ cup fresh blueberries

PREHEAT THE OVEN to 375°F/190°C. Place 12 muffin paper liners in a muffin pan.

SIFT THE FLOUR, baking soda, salt, and half of the allspice into a large mixing bowl. Add 6 tablespoons of the superfine sugar and mix together.

IN A SEPARATE BOWL, whisk the egg whites together lightly. Add the margarine, yogurt, and vanilla extract and mix together well, then stir in the fresh blueberries until thoroughly mixed. Add the fruit mixture to the flour mixture, then gently stir together until just combined. Do not overstir the batter—it is fine for it to be a little lumpy.

DIVIDE THE MUFFIN BATTER evenly among the paper liners (they should be about two-thirds full). Mix the remaining sugar with the remaining allspice, then sprinkle the mixture over the muffins.

BAKE IN THE PREHEATED OVEN for 25 minutes, or until risen and golden. Remove the muffins from the oven and serve warm, or place them on a cooling rack and let cool.

makes 12

lemon & poppy seed muffins

3 cups all-purpose flour

1 tbsp baking powder

heaping $\frac{1}{2}$ cup superfine sugar

2 tbsp poppy seeds

4 tbsp butter

1 extra large egg, beaten

1 cup milk

finely grated rind and juice of

   1 lemon

PREHEAT THE OVEN to 375°F/190°C. Place 12 muffin paper liners in a muffin pan.

SIFT THE FLOUR and baking powder into a large bowl and stir in the sugar.

HEAT A HEAVY SKILLET over medium-high heat and add the poppy seeds. Toast the poppy seeds for about 30 seconds, shaking the skillet to prevent them from burning. Remove from the heat and add to the flour mixture.

MELT THE BUTTER, then beat with the egg, milk, lemon rind, and lemon juice. Pour into the dry mixture and stir well to mix evenly to a soft, sticky dough. Add a little more milk if the mixture is too dry.

SPOON THE MIXTURE into the paper liners, then bake in the preheated oven for 25–30 minutes, or until risen and golden brown. Lift onto a wire rack to cool.

makes 12

double chocolate muffins

PREHEAT THE OVEN to 375°F/190°C. Place 12 muffin paper liners in a muffin pan.

PUT THE BUTTER, superfine sugar, and brown sugar into a bowl and beat well. Beat in the eggs, sour cream, and milk until thoroughly mixed. Sift the flour, baking soda, and cocoa into a separate bowl and stir into the mixture. Add the chocolate chips and mix well.

SPOON THE MIXTURE into the paper liners. Bake in the preheated oven for 25–30 minutes. Remove from the oven and let cool for 10 minutes. Turn out on to a wire rack and let cool completely.

MAKES 12

scant ½ cup butter, softened

scant ¾ cup superfine sugar

½ cup dark brown sugar

2 eggs

⅔ cup sour cream

5 tbsp milk

2 cups all-purpose flour

1 tsp baking soda

2 tbsp unsweetened cocoa

1 cup semisweet chocolate chips

frosted cupcakes

· ·

$^1/_2$ cup butter

heaping $^1/_2$ cup superfine sugar

2 eggs, beaten

1 cup self-rising flour

FROSTING AND DECORATION

$1^3/_4$ cups confectioner's sugar

about 2 tbsp warm water

a few drops of food coloring
    (optional)

sugar flowers, sprinkles, candied
    cherries, and/or chocolate strands,
    to decorate

PREHEAT THE OVEN to 375°F/190°C. Place 16 paper liners into a shallow muffin pan.

PLACE THE BUTTER and sugar in a large bowl and cream together with a wooden spoon or electric mixer until pale and fluffy.

GRADUALLY ADD THE EGGS, beating well after each addition. Fold in the flour lightly and evenly using a metal spoon.

DIVIDE THE MIXTURE among the paper liners and bake in the preheated oven for 15–20 minutes. Cool on a wire rack.

FOR THE FROSTING, sift the confectioner's sugar into a bowl and stir in just enough water to mix to a smooth paste that is thick enough to coat the back of a wooden spoon. Stir in a few drops of food coloring, if using, then spread the frosting over the cupcakes and decorate as desired.

MAKES 16

chocolate butterfly cakes

· ·

1/2 cup butter

1/2 cup superfine sugar

1 1/4 cups self-rising flour

2 eggs

2 tbsp unsweetened cocoa

1 oz/25 g semisweet chocolate,
   melted

confectioners' sugar, for dusting

LEMON BUTTERCREAM

6 tbsp butter, softened

1 1/3 cups confectioners' sugar, sifted

grated rind of 1/2 lemon

1 tbsp lemon juice

PREHEAT THE OVEN to 350°F/180°C. Place 12 paper liners in a shallow muffin pan.

PLACE THE BUTTER, superfine sugar, flour, eggs, and cocoa in a large bowl, and beat with an electric mixer until the mixture is just smooth. Beat in the melted chocolate.

SPOON THE MIXTURE into the paper liners, filling them three-quarters full. Bake in the preheated oven for 15 minutes, or until springy to the touch. Transfer to a wire rack and let cool.

MEANWHILE, make the lemon buttercream. Place the butter in a mixing bowl and beat until fluffy, then gradually beat in the confectioners' sugar. Beat in the lemon rind and gradually add the lemon juice, beating well.

CUT THE TOPS OFF the cakes using a serrated knife. Cut each cake top in half. Spread or pipe the buttercream frosting over the cut surface of each cake and push the 2 cut pieces of cake top into the frosting to form wings. Dust with confectioners' sugar.

MAKES 12

honey & spice cupcakes

PREHEAT THE OVEN to 350°F/180°C. Place paper liners in two 12-cup shallow muffin pans.

PLACE THE BUTTER, sugar, and honey in a large pan and heat gently, stirring, until the butter has melted. Remove the pan from the heat.

SIFT TOGETHER the flour and allspice and stir into the mixture in the pan, then beat in the eggs, mixing to a smooth batter.

SPOON THE BATTER into the paper liners and place a blanched almond on top of each one. Bake in the preheated oven for 20–25 minutes, or until well-risen and golden brown. Transfer to a wire rack to cool.

makes 22-24

²/₃ cup butter

scant ¹/₂ cup light brown sugar

scant ¹/₂ cup honey

1³/₄ cups self-rising flour

1 tsp ground allspice

2 eggs, beaten

22–24 whole blanched almonds

toffee apple cupcakes

....

2 apples

1 tbsp lemon juice

2¼ cups all-purpose flour

2 tsp baking powder

1½ tsp ground cinnamon

heaping ¼ cup light brown sugar

4 tbsp butter, plus extra for greasing

scant ½ cup milk

scant ½ cup apple juice

1 egg, beaten

TOFFEE TOPPING

2 tbsp light cream

3 tbsp light brown sugar

1 tbsp butter

PREHEAT THE OVEN to 400°F/200°C. Grease a 12-cup muffin pan (preferably nonstick).

CORE AND COARSELY GRATE one of the apples. Slice the remaining apple into ¼ inch/5 mm thick wedges and toss in the lemon juice. Sift together the flour, baking powder, and cinnamon, then stir in the sugar and grated apple.

MELT THE BUTTER and mix with the milk, apple juice, and egg. Stir the liquid mixture into the dry ingredients, mixing lightly until just combined.

SPOON THE MIXTURE into the prepared muffin pan. Put two apple slices on top of each cake.

BAKE IN THE PREHEATED OVEN for 20–25 minutes, or until risen, firm, and golden brown. Run a knife around the edge of each cake to loosen, then turn out onto a wire rack to cool.

FOR THE TOFEE TOPPING, place all the ingredients in a small pan and heat, stirring, until the sugar has dissolved. Increase the heat and boil rapidly for 2 minutes, or until slightly thickened and syrupy. Cool slightly, then drizzle over the cakes and let set.

MAKES 12

scones

3½ cups all-purpose flour, plus extra
    for dusting
½ tsp salt
2 tsp baking powder
4 tbsp butter
2 tbsp superfine sugar
1 cup milk, plus extra for glazing
strawberry preserves and whipped
    heavy cream, to serve

PREHEAT THE OVEN to 425°F/220°C.

SIFT THE FLOUR, salt, and baking powder into a bowl. Rub in the butter using your fingertips until the mixture resembles breadcrumbs. Stir in the sugar. Make a well in the center and pour in the milk. Stir in using a spatula to form a soft dough.

TURN THE MIXTURE onto a floured surface and lightly flatten the dough until it is of an even thickness, about ½ inch/1 cm. Don't be heavy-handed; scones need a light touch.

CUT OUT THE SCONES using a 2½-inch/6-cm cookie cutter and place on a cookie sheet.

GLAZE WITH A LITTLE MILK and bake in the preheated oven for 10–12 minutes, until golden and well risen. Cool on a wire rack and serve freshly baked with strawberry preserves and whipped heavy cream.

makes 10-12

rock cakes

PREHEAT THE OVEN to 400°F/200°C. Lightly grease 2 cookie sheets.

SIFT THE FLOUR and baking powder into a large bowl and rub in the butter using your fingertips until it resembles fine breadcrumbs. Stir in the light brown sugar, mixed dried fruit, and lemon rind.

BEAT THE EGG LIGHTLY with a tablespoon of the milk and stir into the flour mixture, adding a little more milk if necessary, until it starts to bind together to form a moist but firm dough.

SPOON SMALL HEAPS of the mixture onto the prepared cookie sheets. Sprinkle with the raw brown sugar.

BAKE IN THE PREHEATED OVEN for 15–20 minutes, or until golden brown and firm. Use a metal spatula to transfer the cakes onto a wire rack to cool.

MAKES 8-10

2 cups all-purpose flour

2 tsp baking powder

$1/2$ cup butter, plus extra
 for greasing

$1/3$ cup light brown sugar

$1/3$ cup mixed dried fruit

finely grated rind of 1 lemon

1 egg

1–2 tbsp milk

2 tsp raw brown sugar